THE LOUDEST HONEY

LYLA BUTLER

First edition.

ISBN: 9781949342406

Cover Design by Derrick Brown

Interior Layout by Nikki Steele

Edited by Wess Mongo Jolley

Proofread by Wess Mongo Jolley

Author Photo by Amy Carlson

Birch Bench Press

birchbenchpress.com

THE LOUDEST HONEY

CONTENTS

FOREWORD

LYLA

Lightning bolts, worlds blooming, and boundless oceans all populate the lush and uncommonly accomplished poetry of Lyla Forest Butler. The multiple time Walt Whitman Birthplace Association Poetry Award honeree feels the perfect literary descendant to Whitman, with her yearning and sometimes eerie observations of a world you won't believe she's only occupied a mere fifteen years. Lyla, too, has the soul of a renegade and a deep social consciousness, but comparisons to other poets will stop there since I'd rather she not feel like the newer version of anything but herself.

The first time I saw her I was transfixed by a tiny girl in the front row of the school choir. She was doing everything in her power to contain herself and her seven-year-old body failed all attempts to be still. One leg betrayed her by madly keeping a beat and I couldn't decide what captivated me more; her palpable need to bust out and dance, or all the obvious effort she was putting into not drawing focus. She clearly was infused with something unique, an unstoppable energy that could barely contain her and vice versa.

Lyla explodes with honesty. She has authenticity that can't be faked. Her sweetness and purity come through in the verse, but it all feels entirely unself-consciousness, she writes with a sincerity that feels subversive from a teenager in this moment in time. In the gorgeous "Ocean, My Ocean" that purity builds on itself:

> Your shells are ancient
>
> they are ruins of a lost world
>
> & gifts to the land dwellers
>
> though we are merely mooncalves
>
> you keep giving
>
> you never stop
>
> & you are mine

The poem has a sensuality and directness that show her at her finest, her most moving. As warm and expansive as that poem is, Lyla's writing is not without a sly humor, as in the wry lament, "Period":

> ...everyone I knew would give me dirty looks
>
> they would laugh nervously
>
> they seemed ashamed of me
>
> embarrassed at my mention of a function of my body
>
> though of course, they'd mention if I sneezed.

This poem, like so many others in the collection, feel so personal that you can't believe it isn't buried in a mountain of sarcasm or cleverness. It's her straightforwardness in concert with an earnest, almost romantic regard for the world that shocks me, as in "Mama":

> The daughter already
>
> an unweeded wildflower

shooting poisonous glances at her mother

eyes blazing like a tippler

There is such an honesty to this poem, and others, like "Storms", and "August Teens"

she is perdition and beguiling and an empress

she is a vice

and you are infatuated

She lets you in and does not pull the rug away; a poet who takes for granted that you, like her, are without a flip or meanspirited bone. By inviting you into the soul and mind of a girl with so much empathy and such a serious lack of pose, you can't help but want to understand, and if you can't, you're happy for her to teach you. In the dizzy freedom of 'Rag Dolling" she takes us to an amusement park, and the sharp turns and lovely sensation of weightlessness are matched within the unexpected rhythm of the verse:

it's more gentle than anticipated

a mother hypnotizing twenty-five babies, all strapped

helpless to

some alien machine on doomsday

but then we climb higher

the ride swoops fast when it nears the ground and

then back up again to full height

weightless, rag-dolling for a beautiful moment,

the horizon

vertical

I don't know how she can possess that amount of confidence in her writing without ever posing or showing off, but she manages the same trick in being herself. Lyla gives me a sense of relief with not only her poetry but her relationship to poetry and the world itself. I spent many afternoons with her at the beginning of the pandemic in an alley in Brooklyn. We sat on chairs placed at safe distances, taking off our masks to read poems of our own or ones we loved. When she'd begin one of her own it seemed her entire countenance shifted and suddenly, she could be anywhere in time, with her writing also striving for a universality first and not a category; as though she never wanted to wow you as much as offer her open hand in hopes you'd take it.

I'm thrilled Lyla writes, but I'm even more amazed that she manages to exist in the world with the same graciousness she displays in her writing. I'll try not to place undue pressure by saying she gives me hope for the future, but I feel so lucky whenever I see her take out a piece of paper and say, "I'd like to read you one of mine." I don't know if she's at a moment where grown-ups continually ask her if she wants to be a poet when she gets older, but the answer hardly matters when she's having such enormous success as one now. I can't wait to see what she writes and accomplishes throughout her life, not only because of her pure heart, but also from what so joyfully pours out of it and into her pen, a gift that should be celebrated and engaged with; held closely in your hands and marveled at, just like this book.

-**Mary Louse Parker**, author *Dear Mr. You*, actress, *Weeds*, *West Wing*

"I like to be a free spirit. Some don't like that, but that's the way I am."

-Diana, Princess of Wales

For Mama—
I kept my promise!
xx

-Bunny

INSTRUCTIONS

open your eyes
good morning
take a deep breath and stretch
listen for the mourning doves
as they slowly pull you
into consciousness
feel the moment in your fingertips

walk out of your house
the sky may be cloudy
or cold rain may seep down your back
and crowd your shoes
do not let it stop you

turn right on the corner that leads
into a dead-end alley
the one with decaying cobblestone
there lurks a black cat
that peers at you with a human gaze
and yellow eyes that shine at night
ask him about his life
he will answer in a heavy and
indistinguishable accent
he will give you a silver key

slip through the gates covered in ivy
trespass on the looming
abandoned house
the one with cracks snaking across its surface
use the key on the rusty old lock to the
deceased garden

run through the tall weeds never stopping
even when they itch your ankles

you will find the pavement again
through a small gap in the garden's fence

continue slowly
down the pavement as far as you can until it
slowly dribbles
away into country
leave your shoes at the end of the pavement
walk barefoot through the spring grass
pick a bouquet of violets—
no one is watching

it is almost sunset now
the lightning bugs are toeing the twilight air
like thirteen-year-olds at a friday night dance
there is a sapling
growing
at the end of the field
run to it!
you are losing the light

listen to the deer
heed their advice
crusade over the mountain
do not look back

there is a little house
it is flaming crackling blazing
the door is still intact
open it
there you will find me
sitting in a chair
i'll be waiting
with open arms
i always have been

KID

they say I'm
too old
for the glowing stars
that pepper my ceiling
strange green aliens
somehow comforting

for chocolate milk
muddy puddles
for the stuffed animals
who know all my deepest secrets
and my sweetest longings

for my own mama
and for big old kisses
who makes the rules?
who says I'm too old
for hide-and-seek
too grown up
to wrestle with my brother
to ask for help
to make mistakes?

who makes the rules?
oh, tell me soon
so I may run
through houses and streets and parks
and make them change the rules

I am never
too old

AUGUST TEENS

golden air in your ears
heat lightning and sparklers
hot as your petulant temper
sunscreen left on a shelf, collecting dust
they wonder why their cheeks
are scalded and a toddler shade of pink
lifeguards & laughs
that taste like honeycomb
failing miserably at fishing
but persevering every day
cities melt
lemonade stands count their quarters

running through a world of suffocating orange
living for the whisper of a breeze that comes
once every blue moon
vexing sisters, scrapes on knees
climbing big old oaks
writing on birch bark

suddenly you catch something on your line
ogling at eyes that resemble your beloved green sea
a girl with undeniable panache
and hair red like the evening sun
she owns the zeitgeist of the seventies
as if it were her own allowance
her whole being is red
she is perdition and beguiling and an empress
she is a vice and
you are infatuated

your dad sneaks little pieces of advice
into every interaction
lately saying that
you are starting to let the sunshine see you

your world is blooming for the first time
and for once, you are not embarrassed
you drink up the sunshine
like it is your sister's fifty-cent lemonade

little secrets are scattered, stars
you form a spider-silk plan
fragile, but there
muster up the courage
and whisper sweetly in her ear:
if you hold my hand
dripping with sweat i
'll kiss you behind the pool house

red girl agrees
she follows, silent
you wonder if her heart is doing gainers too
as you stare into those eyes like a typhoon
crouching on forget-me-nots

stealthy bees appear, brothers
annoying and in your hair
and hornets, more threatening
more like great-aunts
less frequent, but still existing

discovering your diary has been torn though
sobbing furious tears until you have cried a little ocean
you build yourself a boat of paper
and you row far,
far away far from red girl
resting for moments on the scattered islands you pass
all the way into September.

PERIOD.

after i got my period for the very first time
it was like the ocean was inside me
i wanted to let it out, breathe
but it kept churning, a microscopic hurricane
wind at 64 knots

i would talk about it
i would joke about it

i would be endlessly interested
in the new load my body had shouldered
a load not so easy to bear
and don't people usually joke about
the hard things?

but everyone I know would give dirty looks
they would laugh nervously
they seemed ashamed of me
embarrassed at my mention of a function of my body
though, of course, they'd mention if I sneezed

it was heartbreaking
realizing this was not okay
i stopped talking about it

if it was ever mentioned
it would be
in hushed whispers
door closed
remarking on how horrible it was
how vile it was how gross

recently a boy asked how he could help
if i was on my period and needed comfort
it was the first time i had ever heard one

mention the word
unless it was discussing sentence structure
in english
"period"
why was that the first time?

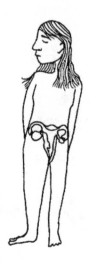

ANXIOUS

sometimes you forget to breathe
you are teetering on violin e-strings
about to snap under your feet

seeping in like spilled india ink
pricking
always
like the stick-n-poke that's half-finished on her ankle—
she said that it hurt
and she can handle pain
it must have been a nightmare

growing like a neglected mess of thorns
in the peeling house's backyard
leaving red marks dancing along your tired arms
when you try to cut it down

snaking into a good day
the beautiful green flash at sunset only awakening
the sickening eels in your stomach
your infected fingers tapping the table
wishing you could sit on the swelling feeling
like you can on your fidgeting hands

it's the feeling of forgetting
of sinking into a murky mariana trench
of piles becoming mountains
you are not an alpinist!
you're just a kid inside.

MAMA

we all nursed somewhere
maybe not on mother's milk
but raised from the earth
bit by bit
seed, sprout, and sapling
someone was there with a watering can

somehow, every relationship
between a mother and a daughter
has umpteen layers
more than is ever discussed

a daughter is born
her mother is her gardener
she is a golden ray of good
the daughter grows
the mother takes only a moment's blink away

but she looks back too late
the daughter already
an unweeded wildflower
shooting poisonous glances at her mother
eyes blazing like a tippler
every breath her mother takes

makes her feel sick
makes her want to run to the end of the world
but the arms she wants to run to
are the same ones she now loathes
the same hands that wiped her tears
and stroked her hair for years

this is the most ferocious painful beautiful love
in the world
daughter to mother, mother to daughter

FOR THE ONE I LOVE

ocean, my ocean
you boundless & beautiful
hungry & wild soul
untamed
mother, home, lullaby
as little girls
we looked up to you
confident like our mamas
& beautiful & mysterious like our own minds
you hold the world tight
in tired arms
arms which toiled
though wars, through destruction
abuse, torture, starvation
& salty tears
but still those arms
are full of love
so much love
You are unafraid & you are mine.

ocean, my ocean
your waves are like butterflies
in the stomachs of young lovers
or perhaps
a curl in a baby's hair
your waves persist
though they are filled
with things that hurt your mighty heart
with plastic bags & soda cans
& with the hate of humankind
but still you keep going
never giving up
you are fearless & fierce
frightful fun & flighty seagulls
You are so much love

& you are mine.

ocean, my ocean
your blue cities & your world of green
symphonies of the nautical kingdom
protector of the secret hideaways
where mermaids pore over their whimsy newspapers
& sea-dragons gather their share of food
your shells are ancient
they are ruins of a lost world
& gifts to the land-dwellers
Though we are merely mooncalves
you keep giving
you never stop
& you are mine.

RAG-DOLLING

you can scream
you can shout
but you can't get out!
bounces around the lines and the minds
of kids like it's the last call they'll ever hear
sweaty hands strangling the tourniquet of a
seatbelt, the harness, a life-saver
preventing a skull-cracking demise

i only got on because the lunch deep down
in my gut had settled, but now i'm not so sure about it
we start to swing, dancing all together, suspended in midair
    balancing on cobweb-thin trust for the ride-makers

it's more gentle than anticipated
a mother hypnotizing twenty-five babies, all strapped helpless to
some alien machine on doomsday

but then we climb higher
the ride swoops fast when it nears the ground and
then back up again to full height
weightless, rag-dolling for a beautiful moment,
the horizon
vertical

BUTTON

1
to be afraid of buttons
to be choked away by those nefarious...
things!
confronting you everywhere you look—
koumpounophobia
is not an irrational fear

2
hands immersed in
the woman's
button collection
every one the same
she's particular with them—
smooth, round, shiny and red

3
my dog ate a button
my parents made a big deal of it
saying he would go to doggy heaven
but the button plopped out
coffee-colored instead of its original shining red
landing on the floor, exhausted
along with the rest of my homework he had eaten

4
amid the backstage whispers
the girl's vest button
snags
on the cabinet door
tumbling to the ground and rolling underneath
the low-hanging shelves
and is forgotten for decades
collecting dust by a shoebox

5

the raggedy ann doll with the beautiful
button eyes
was so fiercely loved
that she was missing multiple limbs:
two arms and her left leg

6

the father knew nothing about sewing
but her bear was missing
a coat button
as his tiny daughter's body shook with sobs
he knew he would find a way to fix it
his massive, cracked hands
fumbling with a microscopic needle

7

a red car blasting obnoxious pop
and toxic teenage gossip
speeds over a button in the street
it doesn't crack

8

the button skids across the table like a rocket:
the perfect hockey puck

9

the girl sewed the golden button
onto her catholic school uniform
a tiny victory!

10

young love
is like a button
plastic, hard and full of holes

WHERE I DREAM

a clear, sunny blue sky
sewn together by white, puffy clouds
which tasted like marshmallows—
that is the blanket I sleep under.

a warm, firm beach full of sand
and, every once in a while,
a child's masterpiece palace, washed away—
that is the mattress I sleep on.

some old, funny seagull
and a few fish that loved the waves—
they are enough to keep me company.

a collection of rocks covered in algae and moss
a spot of solitude, where the ocean stirs, still barely audible—
that is the place where I dream.

BUTTERFLY

lacy, perhaps delicate
flutter into my eyes
ghostly
and purple

painted maypole, you flip
& run from the wind
fragile as a cobweb
but not in spirit—
you are a firecracker
landing in my hand
the strawberry's envy

you shy girl
timid at tea but not in the garden
you perch on your daisy
legs daintily crossed
a proper lady
and when the moon hangs high
like a pearl in the dark night's deep sea
you dance with fireflies

tickle my hair
with fragile fingertips
wispy whisper
say "i love you" to night breezes
birds singing in the sycamore trees
dream little dreams of you

LIGHTNING BOLT

i've always wanted one—
a shock in the fingertips
blue glow flooding my face in the dark rain
i could hold
the prickly thorns of zap
crackling whispers to tell me goodnight
it would tell me of its bravest battles
of soaking indigo nights
over the atlantic
the way it laughs, nefarious
when little girls cry at its dances
the king of mystery
who once struck fear in my heart like a
nightmare
with a friend in those fiery branches of current
maybe i'd be all-knowing
i'd be lightning in a bottle
i'd be power and light
like new love

"YOU'RE REALLY HERE…"

you're really here
tears & arms
flesh & bone

your hair
pink cheeks for days
like orchids
blooming after a long winter
far from the sun

warm embrace
after so long
in your arms

swallowing warm sobs
I am overcome
I am in the world of gold
Dorothy in Oz, maybe

I am far from this body
oh, I am floating on the weightless
wings of doves

I am king
I could kiss you
(I won't)

I never thought I could return
& yet
in flesh & bone

Reunited

AMY LYNN

she walks with unshakable confidence
no, not even that—it's
titanic
mammoth
monumental
the way she walks
the attention she commands is unmistakable
breaking the ground where she steps
the ground she graces

her electric blue eyes pierce
the people
lucky enough to gaze into them
they are everything blue
and everything beautiful
they are lightning and lust
and oceans and lakes
and kisses
and blue moons

when she talks
with the molten blaze
of her quick-witted jokes
and free-falling laugh
everyone stares
they couldn't help it if they tried
the elephant
is in the room

CROW

shrill & piercing & murder
keep my gaze
only on your seductive feathers
stop hiding in the trees

you infect them
with your black illness
you are masses of scream
you are a sea of ravenous cold

lend me a sole feather
let it be softer than your soul
escape the cage
free your spirit
little bird inside

WANDERING ERATICALLY

the beginnings of a forest
start to peek out from their timid hiding spots
the trees surround you with their massive darkness whispering
    always
the eyes following you are surely attached to bodies
that you don't want to see

a castle on a hill interrupts your path
yellow flags flip and flutter in the wind
leaving trails of golden dust behind them
the sun beats down
slipping into cracks and corners
making the world slow down

a sailboat dips and dives
on the verge of submersion
the ocean bats at it like a cat
the stormy sky arguing with the wind
squid ink dots the sea
white stripes are painted across it by the wind's hand
the waves turn restlessly in their sleep

ghosts fly around you
follow you
searching for some form of life to grasp
their lost souls wander erratically
just like you will when
your bones become brittle
and the battered gray pigeons who eat your breakfast
are your only acquaintances
when you are no more than a shell
of the ferocious boy you once were

TO LEAP, MY LOVE

Gusts wail
into the far corners of the night
a whipping wind whirls
& whistles in the winter air
faster, faster.

She leaps over snow & silver symphonies
of the sickening storm of winter
the sorrowful trees that suffer
watch her race against time
faster, faster.

Pounding the earth like lightning
she can see the lovely lilies ahead
& golden laughter
the dancing children of the sun
off she goes
to leap, my love
faster, faster.

Trembling with trepidation
she canters across turbulent fields
there are timid breezes up ahead
away from these tumbling tornadoes
faster, faster.

She is nearing the edge
the flames of her spirit keep her warm
& the wind howls after her
she's not afraid
faster & faster & faster
she leaps into the new day
landing softly in the heart of spring.

MISCHIEF

M
honey and the morning
overflowing orange tea kettle filled to the top
sweltering feet
dance on the burning wood as

I
fumble for my silver keys alone
on the midnight block
city almost asleep c
old, cold wind tastes like
velvet and licorice and the power outage

S
a sigh into her tiny handkerchief e
mbroidered with little crowns
as mischief with the jewelry box unfolds
little green pearls
snake across the smooth floor

C
crawling among the
little muddy piglets
straw hat scrapes against the chipped
sunrise door
and a cartwheel

H
the snapping of elastic and
worn down black tires
a blinding yellow light
in a blinding dark room
springy breeze
& scraping knees on the pavement

I
glistening diamonds in the fading purple light
mysterious fingers
whispering behind tulle curtains
a stained chain

E
an old knight on a rusty black horse
quiet just before dawn
the smell of cinnamon and a woman
singing in her bathroom
in the warm glow of sun-baked sand
toes engulfed

F
wandering through a virgin forest
tiny footsteps
bare green, smelling of old books
the eye of an infant

TINTINNABULATION

why are some of the most beautiful things
given to those who are gone?

when i was little i adored
cemeteries
ancient moss seeping into swooping letters on headstones
the maze of gray, difficult to navigate
a city three feet tall

cantering over the peaceful little plots a
necropolis of sleeping people and aching bones
i stumbled upon a boy's grave
marble with a beautiful heart carved out
so much heavy stone for a tiny body

mama, i want one just like that—
but this boy has died to get his—
well, mama, make sure i get one if i do—
i will, sweetheart, but please don't—
don't what?
die

my smile faded for a moment
does it sting like a wasp?
i envied the beat-up toy trucks positioned
perfectly around the grass guarded the stone
i made a list of toys i wanted there, favorites
to guard my eternal resting place

couldn't I have a grave just for one day?
and then go back to the room I share
with my baby brother
jumping on beds in my cinderella dress?

a may breeze and the whisper of church bells the only
sounds sweeping through the
big sunny boneyard
roots snaking up from my fingertips
blooming into oxeye daisies six feet above

THEM

i watch them interrupt
i watch them gaze
and narrow
and furrow

i watch them yell
i watch them punch
and cry
and bleed

i watch them take
i watch them make us scared
and rape
and ruin

they will shame
and they will point
but you are bigger than them

do not let them take your laugh
your smiling, big, beautiful
open-mouthed laugh
do not stifle it with a hand
just be

the men will never understand

C TRAIN

people from every corner of the world
slip down spotted gray stairs
late for everything
her work, his therapist, her lunch
rip out your metro card—
yours is a one-ride—
slide it down the silver
overused & old
slot—but my apologies
please swipe again
glide through filthy turnstile lasers
take out your earbuds
and hearken to the orchestra
of rats & rails
screeching in perfect harmony t
he bugles of a metropolis
they announce the arrival
of the only train that stops
at Lafayette Avenue
and you know it must be yours
so more stairs
& steel drum thrumming
& heart racing
& toddlers whining
& old friends laughing

PIGEON

perching on a peeling park bench
the gleaming green paint
merely a memory
white specks dot cement cities
gliding through the concrete jungle
lampposts are trees
the buskers' songs
the soul-numbing roars of lions
its bruised wings
make an effort to fly
and as it takes off
a single sick, filthy feather
floats down to the ground
a toddler waddles over to it
eager to thrust it into his mouth

ANALOG

i like things analog
far away from the deadly blue light
not only my fingertips turn them on
but switches
dials and buckles and hair-thin needles
jagged edges
smooth round records with grooves
a race track for tom thumb

i like buttons
i like the crackly buzz on tapes
the shiny little CDs covered in scratches
echoing tiny rainbows in the sun

as complicated routines become
merely taps and swipes
i gather more of my analog things
i crave the feeling
of running my hands over their leathery cases
flooring the gas on a deserted freeway
zipping off into the horizon
knowing i did it myself

COMING TO YOU LIVE!

there's something special about theaters
velvet seats like pews
the arching ceilings,
big chandeliers smiling down at your little body
wandering down an aisle, a big goof
or maybe it's a black-box
a submarine ready to submerge in the big
boundless ocean of words that is this show
the buzz of people, electric energy shocking you
the shared experience leaves you speechless
little moments of love fill your entire being
conductors going over the score with the percussionist sometimes
you're lucky if you catch those

there's something special about theaters
worthy of genuflection
something breathtaking
there's no anticipation like it
being able to drink up the
hard work of real people
not up on the silver screen,
flashing,
racing to grasp your attention

it's right there
just ten feet ahead

JITTERBUG

he brought his old transistor radio
with a giddy expression on his face
his eyes already
dancing
covered in an unshakable spirit
setting it down at a precarious spot
on a countertop long as an old man's beard
he let out
a laughing breath
laced with scorching whiskey

rainy was an understatement
this was nearly a hurricane
of course
only he had cared to visit
the tiny roadside diner
in the loneliest town in the world
but in tumbled a young woman
arms hugging her glossy yellow raincoat
looking distraught in every way
her hair was splayed in all directions
she had screamed
an argument with the wind
worse than any
even with her diabolical mother
and the creases in her forehead increased
the longer she stood in the door
dripping
like a child that had fallen into a fountain

her eyes immediately spotted the man
grinning at her from the bar
she winced
images
of confrontation racing through her mind

she didn't want anything unwanted
from him
the man's eyes softened
a pitiful expression on his face
she kept her razor-sharp gaze on him
but felt a little less frozen
the man turned to an aproned bartender
and muttered something quieter than she would have
guessed he was capable of
then jumping up from the counter
moving with the vigor of a frog on a scorching day
hopping from rock to rock

he turned sharply to his radio
switched it on
and elvis streamed through the speakers
wrapping the man in glee
he relished the moment
gliding around the room
drumming on tables with invisible diners s
ashaying all the way to where she stood
he tapped the woman gently on the shoulder:
"wouldn't you like to dance?"
she beamed

this is what she lives for

THE BROWN BEAR

my dad
always two steps behind
still snoring, a cuddly hibernating bear
lumbers past
when we've had a whole day already
on a perpetual wild goose chase

we face-palm when he's dutifully
searching for the keys
when we're already waiting for him
in our car

i see him meandering in my shadow as i walk
he's going to be left in the dust someday
his sluggish brain just a breath behind
for our fast-paced existence
i still love him, though

LAMENT

january is an endless void of cold
a gray eternity in which everything dies
umbrellas tucked in a corner
a crumpled-up newspaper
plastic bags
catching on departed trees
then ripping into shreds
unable to stand the shrill call of the wind
almost like a harpy
calling out in the dark purgatory
small unmarked graves shudder in the frost
animals hibernate
humans merely sleep
a mother
laments the skeleton of a baby bird fallen from its nest
maybe robins will attend its funeral
but birds don't have funerals anyway
somewhere
buried under mountains of frostbite
masked by clouds and shapeless coats
frozen fingertips purple
with disappointment
and heartbreak and tears
there is a yellow sun
but even it is too weak
for the impenetrable outcry of souls in winter

"SHE WAS INSPIRED…"

she was inspired
with an unshakeable sense of confidence
buttoning up her coat, blue velvet
she noticed a paper snowflake
that was stuck absent-mindedly to the
dirty window
she took it
she was on a mission
she tiptoed past her snoring brother
past the dogs that could tear her to pieces
if they were awake
and past the lock on the bedroom door (she picked it)
as the snow piled up outside
like wool from a freshly sheared lamb
careless and uninviting
as everyone retreated under the covers
from the incoming storm
she turned up her collar and opened the door
she looked for snowflakes in the blizzard
she listened for music in the cracking branches
she found peace in the hungry wind
and sat down with a mug of earl grey

VOYEUR

haven't you always wondered what happens
behind slammed doors
and curtains ripped shut
and in the heads of lovers
when they sleep?

i am a thief
i am addicted
to the adrenaline
of being bad
sneaking into unlocked houses just to
try to piece together
the phantom fingers
that knit with these needles
tired hands that wash with this soap
tired feet that live in these cracked shoes

of peeking
under covers
of beds
diaries
manholes
everywhere
memorizing the loops in the teenage cursive
that weep of loneliness
imagining that I could be that person for her
if I was brave enough
to really face people

i can't stop
i can explain exactly why
i've turned it over in my head
for hours and hours
i do it
just to attempt to grasp that mystery

of humanity
and how things come to be
to understand cause and effect
trying to figure things out
for the day when I really
truly
talk to another soul

ISOLATION

isolation covered his face like a shawl
chipping away at the cracked skin on his palms
his tired eyes passed over portraits of dead relatives
his slippered feet disturbing the perfect silence
he wandered through his empty house
furniture covered in sheets
to protect from the dust bunnies
his only way outside
through a pair of windows
stuck shut for decades
he could only peek through them
if he pushed through the precarious piles
of moldy, dusty takeout

the only living thing in the deceased house
was a single, ineffable
passionately red amaryllis
in bewitching bloom
from a seed planted in March
it had been almost a year

it had been watered
by the overbearing cracks in the ceiling
and had grown by the light
of the beguiling sun
a survivor

he felt the urge
to rip out all of its petals
to snatch its life away
from this gray purgatory
when he realized
he had forgotten how to smile

STORMS

i want the kind of love
that will carry me away
in a sweep of blushing
gasping for air
the kind that will leak into my dreams
spill over my every thought
staining the pages of my books with music

i want what everyone has
i want storybook love, unattainable love
to have an "our song"
hands in jean pockets, safety
someone who tells me that i am like "penny lane"

i want my stomach to turn
i want it to burn my heart, i want to be heartbroken
to give everything to someone just to see it thrown away
for my hands to be held, to be kissed back
when you're in love, life is more precious
time is shorter, fruit tastes sweeter
even if it ends in broken glass, you lived beautifully

i want to get hurt, to run to it, to work for it
to get my heart shattered and cut my fingers
on the broken pieces
to learn why storms are named after people
to write some love poem that will be
memorized

i want to wail like a baby on its first night in the world
stupid and in someone's loving arms
becoming a storm, my thunderclaps heard
my name immortal

"THERE IS A PAINTING..."

there is a painting
hanging in an ancient house
at the end of the world

a tired frame
amidst countless others
just as lonely and just as forgotten
an old woman stands memorizing
the familiar brush strokes before her
that seem almost alive

the colors reflecting in her heartbroken eyes
eyes that used to carry a whisper of hope
that slowly dwindled away
the end of a candle
dancing with fragments of her
little life
a life long gone
a life that thinned to ancient paper
then fraying thread a
nd then to dust
she steps closer to the frame

a lighthouse breaking through the fog—
a friend used to say that on foggy days
though everyone felt gray and broken
the lighthouse was the only one over the moon
he could finally do his job
sunburnt shoulders
tender heels resting in the shade
umbrellas blooming open against the harsh wind
constricted breaths in that quiet moment
that beautiful
terrifying moment

before the exhilarating embrace
of the approaching waves

ABOUT THE AUTHOR

Lyla Forest Butler is a lover of life, native of Brooklyn, and poet. She won the Walt Whitman Birthplace Association Student Poetry Contest for three years in a row and has also received other awards for her writing, including a gold key in the Scholastic Art & Writing Awards and the UNIS Student Haiku Contest in 2018. Lyla is a student at Saint Ann's School. Lyla lives with her parents, her little brother, two French bulldogs and a cat. In her spare time, Lyla loves to do theater, play softball, karate, art, and music.

ACKNOWLEDGMENTS

Thank you so much to Derrick Brown and Nikki Steele for all their hard work in helping me put this out, and a special thanks to my parents and my little brother.

The untitled poem ("there is a painting…") was written in collaboration with the lovely Alice Rosenberg and Sonja Seidman. I adore you.

And lastly, thank YOU for picking up this book! I'm so honored that something in my crazy brain made it to yours.

All my love,

Lyla

CPSIA information can be obtained
at www.ICGtesting.com
Printed in the USA
LVHW052305031121
702364LV00005B/185